My Camping Journal ⛺

Kids
Camping
JOURNAL

Memories Forever

NAME: _____

©The Life Graduate Publishing Group

No part of this book may be scanned, reproduced or distributed in any printed or electronic form without the prior permission of the author or publisher.

My Camping Journal

JOURNAL SECTIONS

01 Camping Journal

Record all of your details, memories, funny stories and notes from your camping adventures.

02 My Pictures

A section at the back of the journal to stick all of your favorite pictures, photo's or souvenirs. (eg postcards, a leaf, a feather etc.)

OUR CAMPING LOCATION

_____

WE ARRIVED ON __/__/__   **WE DEPARTED ON** __/__/__

WHO CAME CAMPING? List the names of the people with you.
_____
_____

HOW DO YOU LIKE YOUR CAMPSITE?
It's AWESOME!   It's OK.   Not great at this stage...
_____
_____

PLACES WE VISITED AND THINGS WE DID
_____
_____
_____
_____
_____
_____
_____

My Camping Journal

THE BEST THINGS
Anything funny happen?
Any special moments you will remember forever?

___

ANYTHING ELSE.....?
- Names or details of fellow campers or kids to remember for next time?
- Would you bring something along next time to make the trip even better? eg. Bike
- Things you liked or disliked?
- Was WiFi available? How did you like your meals? Did you sleep OK?

___

My Camping Journal

 Use this section to draw a picture or get those with you to write a nice little note about your camping trip!

My Camping Journal

 Use this section to draw a picture or get those with you to write a nice little note about your camping trip!

OUR CAMPING LOCATION

_____

WE ARRIVED ON ___/___/___   **WE DEPARTED ON** ___/___/___

WHO CAME CAMPING? List the names of the people with you.
_____

_____

HOW DO YOU LIKE YOUR CAMPSITE?
It's AWESOME!   It's OK.   Not great at this stage...
_____

_____

PLACES WE VISITED AND THINGS WE DID
_____

_____

_____

_____

_____

_____

_____

My Camping Journal

THE BEST THINGS
Anything funny happen?
Any special moments you will remember forever?

_____
_____
_____
_____
_____
_____
_____

ANYTHING ELSE.....?
- Names or details of fellow campers or kids to remember for next time?
- Would you bring something along next time to make the trip even better? eg. Bike
- Things you liked or disliked?
- Was WiFi available? How did you like your meals? Did you sleep OK?

_____
_____
_____
_____
_____
_____
_____

My Camping Journal

 Use this section to draw a picture or get those with you to write a nice little note about your camping trip!

My Camping Journal

Use this section to draw a picture or get those with you to write a nice little note about your camping trip!

OUR CAMPING LOCATION

_____

WE ARRIVED ON ___/___/___   **WE DEPARTED ON** ___/___/___

WHO CAME CAMPING? List the names of the people with you.

_____

_____

HOW DO YOU LIKE YOUR CAMPSITE?

It's AWESOME!   It's OK.   Not great at this stage...

_____

_____

PLACES WE VISITED AND THINGS WE DID

_____

_____

_____

_____

_____

_____

_____

My Camping Journal

THE BEST THINGS
Anything funny happen?
Any special moments you will remember forever?

_____
_____
_____
_____
_____
_____
_____

ANYTHING ELSE.....?
- Names or details of fellow campers or kids to remember for next time?
- Would you bring something along next time to make the trip even better? eg. Bike
- Things you liked or disliked?
- Was WiFi available? How did you like your meals? Did you sleep OK?

_____
_____
_____
_____
_____
_____
_____
_____

My Camping Journal

 Use this section to draw a picture or get those with you to write a nice little note about your camping trip!

My Camping Journal 🏕

Use this section to draw a picture or get those with you to write a nice little note about your camping trip!

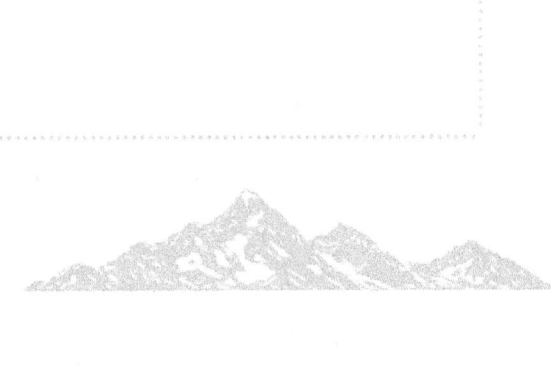

OUR CAMPING LOCATION

_____

WE ARRIVED ON __/__/__   **WE DEPARTED ON** __/__/__

WHO CAME CAMPING? List the names of the people with you.

_____

_____

HOW DO YOU LIKE YOUR CAMPSITE?

It's AWESOME!   It's OK.   Not great at this stage...

_____

_____

PLACES WE VISITED AND THINGS WE DID

_____

_____

_____

_____

_____

_____

_____

My Camping Journal

THE BEST THINGS
Anything funny happen?
Any special moments you will remember forever?

_____
_____
_____
_____
_____
_____
_____

ANYTHING ELSE.....?
- Names or details of fellow campers or kids to remember for next time?
- Would you bring something along next time to make the trip even better? eg. Bike
- Things you liked or disliked?
- Was WiFi available? How did you like your meals? Did you sleep OK?

_____
_____
_____
_____
_____
_____
_____
_____

My Camping Journal

 Use this section to draw a picture or get those with you to write a nice little note about your camping trip!

My Camping Journal 🏕

 Use this section to draw a picture or get those with you to write a nice little note about your camping trip!

OUR CAMPING LOCATION

_____

WE ARRIVED ON ___/___/___   **WE DEPARTED ON** ___/___/___

WHO CAME CAMPING? List the names of the people with you.

_____

_____

HOW DO YOU LIKE YOUR CAMPSITE?

It's AWESOME!   It's OK.   Not great at this stage...

_____

PLACES WE VISITED AND THINGS WE DID

_____
_____
_____
_____
_____
_____
_____

My Camping Journal

THE BEST THINGS — Anything funny happen?
Any special moments you will remember forever?

_____
_____
_____
_____
_____
_____
_____

ANYTHING ELSE.....?
- Names or details of fellow campers or kids to remember for next time?
- Would you bring something along next time to make the trip even better? eg. Bike
- Things you liked or disliked?
- Was WiFi available? How did you like your meals? Did you sleep OK?

_____
_____
_____
_____
_____
_____
_____
_____

My Camping Journal

 Use this section to draw a picture or get those with you to write a nice little note about your camping trip!

My Camping Journal

Use this section to draw a picture or get those with you to write a nice little note about your camping trip!

 My Camping Journal

 **OUR CAMPING LOCATION**

_____

WE ARRIVED ON ___/___/___   **WE DEPARTED ON** ___/___/___

WHO CAME CAMPING? List the names of the people with you.

_____

_____

HOW DO YOU LIKE YOUR CAMPSITE?

It's AWESOME!   It's OK.   Not great at this stage...

_____

_____

PLACES WE VISITED AND THINGS WE DID

_____

_____

_____

_____

_____

_____

_____

My Camping Journal

THE BEST THINGS
Anything funny happen?
Any special moments you will remember forever?

_____
_____
_____
_____
_____
_____
_____

ANYTHING ELSE.....?
- Names or details of fellow campers or kids to remember for next time?
- Would you bring something along next time to make the trip even better? eg. Bike
- Things you liked or disliked?
- Was WiFi available? How did you like your meals? Did you sleep OK?

_____
_____
_____
_____
_____
_____
_____

My Camping Journal

 Use this section to draw a picture or get those with you to write a nice little note about your camping trip!

My Camping Journal 🏕

 Use this section to draw a picture or get those with you to write a nice little note about your camping trip!

OUR CAMPING LOCATION

_____

WE ARRIVED ON __/__/__   **WE DEPARTED ON** __/__/__

WHO CAME CAMPING? List the names of the people with you.

_____

_____

HOW DO YOU LIKE YOUR CAMPSITE?

It's AWESOME!   It's OK.   Not great at this stage...

_____

_____

PLACES WE VISITED AND THINGS WE DID

_____

_____

_____

_____

_____

_____

_____

My Camping Journal

THE BEST THINGS
Anything funny happen?
Any special moments you will remember forever?

_____
_____
_____
_____
_____
_____
_____

ANYTHING ELSE.....?
- Names or details of fellow campers or kids to remember for next time?
- Would you bring something along next time to make the trip even better? eg. Bike
- Things you liked or disliked?
- Was WiFi available? How did you like your meals? Did you sleep OK?

_____
_____
_____
_____
_____
_____
_____
_____

My Camping Journal

 Use this section to draw a picture or get those with you to write a nice little note about your camping trip!

My Camping Journal

Use this section to draw a picture or get those with you to write a nice little note about your camping trip!

OUR CAMPING LOCATION

_____

WE ARRIVED ON __/__/__   **WE DEPARTED ON** __/__/__

WHO CAME CAMPING? List the names of the people with you.

_____

_____

HOW DO YOU LIKE YOUR CAMPSITE?

It's AWESOME!   It's OK.   Not great at this stage...

_____

PLACES WE VISITED AND THINGS WE DID

_____

_____

_____

_____

_____

_____

_____

My Camping Journal

THE BEST THINGS
Anything funny happen?
Any special moments you will remember forever?

_____
_____
_____
_____
_____
_____
_____

ANYTHING ELSE.....?
- Names or details of fellow campers or kids to remember for next time?
- Would you bring something along next time to make the trip even better? eg. Bike
- Things you liked or disliked?
- Was WiFi available? How did you like your meals? Did you sleep OK?

_____
_____
_____
_____
_____
_____
_____

My Camping Journal

 Use this section to draw a picture or get those with you to write a nice little note about your camping trip!

My Camping Journal

 Use this section to draw a picture or get those with you to write a nice little note about your camping trip!

OUR CAMPING LOCATION

_____

WE ARRIVED ON __/__/__   **WE DEPARTED ON** __/__/__

WHO CAME CAMPING? List the names of the people with you.
_____
_____

HOW DO YOU LIKE YOUR CAMPSITE?

It's AWESOME!   It's OK.   Not great at this stage...

_____
_____

PLACES WE VISITED AND THINGS WE DID

_____
_____
_____
_____
_____
_____
_____

My Camping Journal

THE BEST THINGS — Anything funny happen? Any special moments you will remember forever?

_____
_____
_____
_____
_____
_____

ANYTHING ELSE.....?
- Names or details of fellow campers or kids to remember for next time?
- Would you bring something along next time to make the trip even better? eg. Bike
- Things you liked or disliked?
- Was WiFi available? How did you like your meals? Did you sleep OK?

_____
_____
_____
_____
_____
_____

My Camping Journal

 Use this section to draw a picture or get those with you to write a nice little note about your camping trip!

My Camping Journal Use this section to draw a picture or get those with you to write a nice little note about your camping trip!

OUR CAMPING LOCATION

_____

WE ARRIVED ON __/__/__   **WE DEPARTED ON** __/__/__

WHO CAME CAMPING? List the names of the people with you.

_____

_____

HOW DO YOU LIKE YOUR CAMPSITE?

It's AWESOME! ○   It's OK. ○   Not great at this stage... ○

_____

_____

PLACES WE VISITED AND THINGS WE DID

_____

_____

_____

_____

_____

_____

_____

My Camping Journal

THE BEST THINGS
Anything funny happen?
Any special moments you will remember forever?

_____
_____
_____
_____
_____
_____
_____

ANYTHING ELSE.....?
- Names or details of fellow campers or kids to remember for next time?
- Would you bring something along next time to make the trip even better? eg. Bike?
- Things you liked or disliked?
- Was WiFi available? How did you like your meals? Did you sleep OK?

_____
_____
_____
_____
_____
_____
_____
_____

My Camping Journal

 Use this section to draw a picture or get those with you to write a nice little note about your camping trip!

My Camping Journal

Use this section to draw a picture or get those with you to write a nice little note about your camping trip!

OUR CAMPING LOCATION

_____

WE ARRIVED ON __/__/__   **WE DEPARTED ON** __/__/__

WHO CAME CAMPING? List the names of the people with you.

_____

_____

HOW DO YOU LIKE YOUR CAMPSITE?

It's AWESOME!   It's OK.   Not great at this stage...

_____

_____

PLACES WE VISITED AND THINGS WE DID

_____

_____

_____

_____

_____

_____

My Camping Journal

THE BEST THINGS
Anything funny happen?
Any special moments you will remember forever?

_____
_____
_____
_____
_____
_____

ANYTHING ELSE.....?
- Names or details of fellow campers or kids to remember for next time?
- Would you bring something along next time to make the trip even better? eg. Bike
- Things you liked or disliked?
- Was WiFi available? How did you like your meals? Did you sleep OK?

_____
_____
_____
_____
_____
_____
_____

My Camping Journal

 Use this section to draw a picture or get those with you to write a nice little note about your camping trip!

My Camping Journal

Use this section to draw a picture or get those with you to write a nice little note about your camping trip!

OUR CAMPING LOCATION

_____

WE ARRIVED ON __/__/__   **WE DEPARTED ON** __/__/__

WHO CAME CAMPING? List the names of the people with you.

_____

_____

HOW DO YOU LIKE YOUR CAMPSITE?

It's AWESOME!   It's OK.   Not great at this stage...

_____

_____

PLACES WE VISITED AND THINGS WE DID

_____

_____

_____

_____

_____

_____

_____

My Camping Journal

THE BEST THINGS
Anything funny happen?
Any special moments you will remember forever?

_____
_____
_____
_____
_____
_____
_____

ANYTHING ELSE.....?
- Names or details of fellow campers or kids to remember for next time?
- Would you bring something along next time to make the trip even better? eg. Bike
- Things you liked or disliked?
- Was WiFi available? How did you like your meals? Did you sleep OK?

_____
_____
_____
_____
_____
_____
_____

My Camping Journal

 Use this section to draw a picture or get those with you to write a nice little note about your camping trip!

My Camping Journal Use this section to draw a picture or get those with you to write a nice little note about your camping trip!

OUR CAMPING LOCATION

_____

WE ARRIVED ON __/__/__   **WE DEPARTED ON** __/__/__

WHO CAME CAMPING? List the names of the people with you.
_____
_____

HOW DO YOU LIKE YOUR CAMPSITE?

It's AWESOME!   It's OK.   Not great at this stage...
_____

PLACES WE VISITED AND THINGS WE DID
_____
_____
_____
_____
_____
_____
_____

My Camping Journal

THE BEST THINGS — Anything funny happen?
Any special moments you will remember forever?

_____
_____
_____
_____
_____
_____
_____

ANYTHING ELSE.....?
- Names or details of fellow campers or kids to remember for next time?
- Would you bring something along next time to make the trip even better? eg. Bike
- Things you liked or disliked?
- Was WiFi available? How did you like your meals? Did you sleep OK?

_____
_____
_____
_____
_____
_____
_____
_____

My Camping Journal

 Use this section to draw a picture or get those with you to write a nice little note about your camping trip!

My Camping Journal

Use this section to draw a picture or get those with you to write a nice little note about your camping trip!

OUR CAMPING LOCATION

_____

WE ARRIVED ON ___/___/___   **WE DEPARTED ON** ___/___/___

WHO CAME CAMPING? List the names of the people with you.

_____

_____

HOW DO YOU LIKE YOUR CAMPSITE?

It's AWESOME!   It's OK.   Not great at this stage...

_____

PLACES WE VISITED AND THINGS WE DID

_____

_____

_____

_____

_____

_____

_____

My Camping Journal

THE BEST THINGS
Anything funny happen?
Any special moments you will remember forever?

_____
_____
_____
_____
_____
_____
_____

ANYTHING ELSE.....?
- Names or details of fellow campers or kids to remember for next time?
- Would you bring something along next time to make the trip even better? eg. Bike
- Things you liked or disliked?
- Was WiFi available? How did you like your meals? Did you sleep OK?

_____
_____
_____
_____
_____
_____
_____

My Camping Journal

Use this section to draw a picture or get those with you to write a nice little note about your camping trip!

My Camping Journal

 Use this section to draw a picture or get those with you to write a nice little note about your camping trip!

OUR CAMPING LOCATION

_____

WE ARRIVED ON ___/___/___   **WE DEPARTED ON** ___/___/___

WHO CAME CAMPING? List the names of the people with you.

_____

_____

HOW DO YOU LIKE YOUR CAMPSITE?

It's AWESOME!   It's OK.   Not great at this stage...

_____

_____

PLACES WE VISITED AND THINGS WE DID

_____

_____

_____

_____

_____

_____

_____

My Camping Journal

THE BEST THINGS
Anything funny happen?
Any special moments you will remember forever?

_____
_____
_____
_____
_____
_____
_____

ANYTHING ELSE.....?
- Names or details of fellow campers or kids to remember for next time?
- Would you bring something along next time to make the trip even better? eg. Bike
- Things you liked or disliked?
- Was WiFi available? How did you like your meals? Did you sleep OK?

_____
_____
_____
_____
_____
_____
_____
_____

My Camping Journal

 Use this section to draw a picture or get those with you to write a nice little note about your camping trip!

My Camping Journal

Use this section to draw a picture or get those with you to write a nice little note about your camping trip!

OUR CAMPING LOCATION

_____

WE ARRIVED ON __/__/__   **WE DEPARTED ON** __/__/__

WHO CAME CAMPING? List the names of the people with you.
_____

_____

HOW DO YOU LIKE YOUR CAMPSITE?

It's AWESOME!   It's OK.   Not great at this stage...
_____

_____

PLACES WE VISITED AND THINGS WE DID
_____

_____

_____

_____

_____

_____

_____

My Camping Journal

THE BEST THINGS
Anything funny happen?
Any special moments you will remember forever?

_____
_____
_____
_____
_____
_____
_____

ANYTHING ELSE.....?
- Names or details of fellow campers or kids to remember for next time?
- Would you bring something along next time to make the trip even better? eg. Bike
- Things you liked or disliked?
- Was WiFi available? How did you like your meals? Did you sleep OK?

_____
_____
_____
_____
_____
_____
_____

My Camping Journal

 Use this section to draw a picture or get those with you to write a nice little note about your camping trip!

My Camping Journal 🏕

 Use this section to draw a picture or get those with you to write a nice little note about your camping trip!

#

OUR CAMPING LOCATION

_____

WE ARRIVED ON __/__/__   **WE DEPARTED ON** __/__/__

WHO CAME CAMPING? List the names of the people with you.

_____

_____

HOW DO YOU LIKE YOUR CAMPSITE?

It's AWESOME!   It's OK.   Not great at this stage...

_____

_____

PLACES WE VISITED AND THINGS WE DID

_____

_____

_____

_____

_____

_____

_____

My Camping Journal

THE BEST THINGS — Anything funny happen? Any special moments you will remember forever?

_____
_____
_____
_____
_____
_____

ANYTHING ELSE.....?
- Names or details of fellow campers or kids to remember for next time?
- Would you bring something along next time to make the trip even better? eg. Bike
- Things you liked or disliked?
- Was WiFi available? How did you like your meals? Did you sleep OK?

_____
_____
_____
_____
_____
_____
_____

My Camping Journal

Use this section to draw a picture or get those with you to write a nice little note about your camping trip!

My Camping Journal

 Use this section to draw a picture or get those with you to write a nice little note about your camping trip!

OUR CAMPING LOCATION

_____

WE ARRIVED ON ___/___/___ **WE DEPARTED ON** ___/___/___

WHO CAME CAMPING? List the names of the people with you.

_____

_____

HOW DO YOU LIKE YOUR CAMPSITE?

It's AWESOME!   It's OK.   Not great at this stage...

_____

_____

PLACES WE VISITED AND THINGS WE DID

_____

_____

_____

_____

_____

_____

_____

My Camping Journal

THE BEST THINGS
Anything funny happen?
Any special moments you will remember forever?

___

ANYTHING ELSE.....?
- Names or details of fellow campers or kids to remember for next time?
- Would you bring something along next time to make the trip even better? eg. Bike
- Things you liked or disliked?
- Was WiFi available? How did you like your meals? Did you sleep OK?

___

My Camping Journal

 Use this section to draw a picture or get those with you to write a nice little note about your camping trip!

My Camping Journal

Use this section to draw a picture or get those with you to write a nice little note about your camping trip!

#

OUR CAMPING LOCATION

_____

WE ARRIVED ON ___/___/___   **WE DEPARTED ON** ___/___/___

WHO CAME CAMPING? List the names of the people with you.

_____

_____

HOW DO YOU LIKE YOUR CAMPSITE?

It's AWESOME!   It's OK.   Not great at this stage...

_____

_____

PLACES WE VISITED AND THINGS WE DID

_____

_____

_____

_____

_____

_____

_____

My Camping Journal

THE BEST THINGS
Anything funny happen?
Any special moments you will remember forever?

_____
_____
_____
_____
_____
_____
_____

ANYTHING ELSE.....?
- Names or details of fellow campers or kids to remember for next time?
- Would you bring something along next time to make the trip even better? eg. Bike
- Things you liked or disliked?
- Was WiFi available? How did you like your meals? Did you sleep OK?

_____
_____
_____
_____
_____
_____
_____

My Camping Journal

 Use this section to draw a picture or get those with you to write a nice little note about your camping trip!

My Camping Journal 🏕

 Use this section to draw a picture or get those with you to write a nice little note about your camping trip!

OUR CAMPING LOCATION

_____

WE ARRIVED ON __/__/__   **WE DEPARTED ON** __/__/__

WHO CAME CAMPING? List the names of the people with you.

_____

_____

HOW DO YOU LIKE YOUR CAMPSITE?

It's AWESOME!   It's OK.   Not great at this stage...

_____

_____

PLACES WE VISITED AND THINGS WE DID

_____

_____

_____

_____

_____

_____

My Camping Journal

THE BEST THINGS — Anything funny happen?
Any special moments you will remember forever?

_____
_____
_____
_____
_____
_____

ANYTHING ELSE.....?
- Names or details of fellow campers or kids to remember for next time?
- Would you bring something along next time to make the trip even better? eg. Bike
- Things you liked or disliked?
- Was WiFi available? How did you like your meals? Did you sleep OK?

_____
_____
_____
_____
_____
_____
_____

My Camping Journal

02

My Pictures

Stick Your Favorite Pictures or Photo's in Here!

My Camping Journal

 Remember to add details like location, date and time next to each picture, photo or item.

My Camping Journal

 Remember to add details like location, date and time next to each picture, photo or item.

My Camping Journal

 Remember to add details like location, date and time next to each picture, photo or item.

My Camping Journal 🏕

 Remember to add details like location, date and time next to each picture, photo or item.

My Camping Journal

Remember to add details like location, date and time next to each picture, photo or item.

My Camping Journal

 Remember to add details like location, date and time next to each picture, photo or item.

My Camping Journal

 Remember to add details like location, date and time next to each picture, photo or item.

My Camping Journal

Memories Forever

www.ingramcontent.com/pod-product-compliance
Lightning Source LLC
LaVergne TN
LVHW081524060526
838200LV00044B/1995